Divorce Smart

A Dad's Story

How I went from Half to Whole

Dr. Richard Wood

Copyright © 2022 Richard Wood.

Used by permission. All rights reserved.

Disclaimer:
Use this information at your own risk. The author's experiences, thoughts, opinions and observations expressed in this guide are just that, his thoughts, opinions and observations. The author is not a lawyer and does not attest to the lawfulness of any of his actions or advice. The content provided herein are simply for educational purposes and does not take the place of legal advice from an attorney. No liability is assumed for losses, damages, or outcomes due to the information provided. The author is not responsible for the reader's choices, actions, or results.

For information about this title, contact the publisher:
The Bingham Group, LLC
Manlydivorce@gmail.com

1st Edition 2022

Preface

The intent of my story, this guide, is to share how I confronted my greatest fear (divorce) and won.

For many women, the American divorce industry represents the fastest route to financial freedom and independence.

Divorce often strips men of their assets, and for dads it's worse; they can be stripped of their fatherhood.

The years leading up to my divorce were dreadful and all about survival. Then came the day when I learned that my marriage would end. That was the day when I decided my future single-life would be all about thriving.

Divorce became my opportunity to rewrite the narrative; one full of happiness and gratitude.

This guide intermixes my personal stories with universal, how-to strategies, that help men (dads too) through the divorce process.

I'll demonstrate how I worked with the system to achieve an obstacle free, happy, financially sound, and new beginning for me and my sons.

The years leading up to my divorce included marital therapy, couple's retreats etc., but there came a point when it was obvious that my wife wasn't sincere about remaining together; divorce was in my future.

Accepting that there was nothing further I could do to keep my family together caused me to reflect on how I reached that stage.

Reflection brought clarity. I saw that I was so determined to keep my marriage together, and my children in a two-parent household, that I compromised my core principles.

I knew that my marriage was dead for years. However, admitting that meant divorce, and that scared me. As such, I kept my marriage alive by receding into a world of denial. I lied to myself by making believe that with the passage of time, my situation would improve.

By the time I was ready to accept that my marriage was over, my sons and I were no more than actors on a stage. A stage where we did our best to present our family as *normal* to outsiders looking in.

Behind the façade, were five individuals living in great pain.

My wife treated our sons as possessions; never an ounce of empathy or love. We were all subjected to gaslighting. I was emasculated on a daily basis.

Reflecting on our past brought me to tears. However, wallowing in self-pity over past mistakes wouldn't help me, or my children.

I made the decision to leave my past behind by handling my upcoming divorce as a golden opportunity.

My divorce would serve as the transport vehicle that delivered a new and better future to my sons and me.

At that point, I knew nothing about the mechanics of divorce, so I used the time before the inevitable divorce summons to learn all that I could.

I interviewed attorneys, spoke with divorced men and women, read books, and scanned the internet for information.

By the time I was served, I was locked and loaded; ready to fight and win every asset and parental right that was legally possible.

I vividly recall the day when I handed the summons to my attorney.

She greeted me at the door to her office and offered me condolences. I looked at her with a big smile and asked, "Sorry? Are you kidding me? I'm so ready. We got this."

Sixteen months later, three of my four sons and I remained in the marital home with all of our belongings, my cars, horses, retirement savings, and I received child-support.

The only things missing from our lives was stress and an abusive wife and mother. I also used financial strategies that allowed me to profit during and after the divorce.

While the tides are changing for men, fantastic outcomes don't just happen.

My results came about from self-discipline and working hand-in-hand with my attorney.

To the uninitiated, my approach will sound cold and calculated. Take heed, divorce proceedings are not warm and fuzzy, and are in fact, all about the math.

At its core, divorce is an expensive legal proceeding that cuts up and discards men and their families.

Now that I'm on the other side and learned how to maneuver that system, I'm sharing my story and strategies to empower others.

My success was the result of persistent and proper planning, especially in matters of finance, which frankly my wife and her attorney didn't anticipate. I caught them off guard, then while they were busy not knowing how to respond to solid evidence, I went on to achieve a divorce that brought joy back into my life.

Everything presented in this guide comes from my personal experiences and observations while participating in a divorce that took place in New York State. I'm not an attorney, nor am I offering legal advice, or guaranteeing you a result like mine.

Too many men have come to believe there's no use in fighting because most outcomes favor women and moms. This guide demonstrates that fair outcomes are possible.

From this paragraph forward, I'll assume you're facing a long-term break up or divorce.

The best thing you can do for yourself is to hang up your sorrow, disappointment and wishing for a reconciliation. She's no longer your life partner - that all ended the day papers were served.

Now is your time to become a worthy and strong opponent to secure your financial future, and if you have children, secure custody arrangements that you'll deem fair.

It won't be long before you and your partner are unentangled single people. It's important that you prepare yourself for that day.

My goal is to help you retain all that you value so that you'll be emotionally and financially intact on the other side of your divorce; ready for a fresh start.

Your best chance at success is to remain in your marital/shared home until the divorce is final. No worries... I'll demonstrate how to remain home with little conflict.

I'll also show you how to avoid traps, legal nightmares, false accusations, protect what's yours, and win custody (or avoid it) if that's what you seek.

Later, after your divorce is settled, you can set aside time to heal, get counseling, or whatever you need to deal with your past. Use that time to correct your faults so that history doesn't repeat itself.

The years leading up to and throughout my divorce were lonely, but they weren't the first time I had to rely on myself.

At 21 years of age, I decided to become a surgeon. It was all on me - I'd be the first college graduate and physician from my blue-collar family. There was no one to advise or guide me, little moral support, and no financial help. The back story is that I quit high school during 9th grade then returned a year later to obtain my degree 4 years later, graduating near the bottom of my class.

Added to the obvious challenges, was that I was a white male. White males were pushed aside by admissions offices in favor of women and people of color. Minorities were actively recruited and held to much lower academic and personal achievements than me. Many were given free-rides, while I worked 2 to 3 jobs throughout the eight years of college and medical school. In spite of the tremendous odds against me, I made it all the way to attaining a residency at Yale New Haven Hospital.

Reflecting on my past achievements provided the courage that I needed to embrace the struggle. So much so, that I realized achieving a fair divorce outcome would be easier than my past accomplishments – and so it was.

Don't waste this limited time getting caught up in self-pity, trying to fight the system, or looking for support from others that will never come. At this moment, your future is on the line. No one can look out for your future better than you will.

My job as I saw it was helping my judge make decisions in my favor and the process was quite simple.

I hired a lawyer, continued on with my career, and remained actively involved in my son's lives. No drama, just parenting in my usual manner, strategically managing assets, along with collecting and organizing evidence that would support me in a court of law.

I was divorcing a manipulative and deceitful person who was very successful in getting her way by lying and manipulating others - that worried me.

As it turned out, there was nothing to worry about. My wife stuck with her emotional and manipulative strategies, which up against the solid and objective evidence I presented, was a waste of her time.

Judges make rulings on objective data. The litigant who puts that type of data before them, wins.

You'll be up against a court system who views women as sacred and helpless victims. A system that asserts that the best place for children, regardless of the circumstances, is with their moms.

However, there's great news. At the core of this biased system are laws.

Modern laws assert that men and women are equally capable of earning a living to support their families. Except in matters of abortion, father's rights are nearly equivalent to mother's rights.

Your job will be collecting and presenting proper evidence so that members of the court can rule based on the evidence you present, rather than having to resort to their personal biases.

Here's how it plays out…. in the absence of objective evidence from either litigant, the judge, within the confines of the law, will be forced to rule based on their personal opinions, e.g., women are revered queens, mothers are sacred, and men are lowly money machines.

It's your responsibility to avoid a biased ruling.

Between now and D-Day, collect every possible bit of objective evidence that a judge might need, or demand, at your hearing. Then, have that evidence immediately available in triplicates – a copy for you, your opponent and the judge.

Why? Judges love efficiency and fortunately for you, family court judges in particular don't like to prolong cases for purposes of discovery. This means that when you present credible evidence at your hearing, and the other side has nothing to immediately refute it, that the judge is unlikely to postpone the hearing to wait on discovery from your opposition, e.g., they'll make a decision based on the evidence you presented.

Make it easy for your judge to make on the spot decisions that favor you.

Table of Contents

Introduction 1

A Male's Perspective 3

Chapter 1 3

Divorce in Simple Terms 5

Chapter 2 5

The Smiling Warrior 7

Chapter 3 7

Universal Precautions 12

Chapter 4 12

Dress Me Slowly I'm in a Rush 14

Chapter 5 14

Happy Wife, Happy Life 18

Chapter 6 18

Remain in Your Marital Home 20

Chapter 7 20

No One is Perfect 25

Chapter 8	25
Home-Based Strategies	27
Chapter 9	27
Prepare To Be Judged	31
Chapter 10	31
Interim Divorce Home Life	35
Chapter 11	35
Active Participation Matters	38
Chapter 12	38
Divorce Threats	42
Chapter 13	42
The Master of Details Wins	44
Chapter 14	44
Anticipate Betrayals	52
Chapter 15	52
Timing and Money Matters	55
Chapter 16	55
Children and Custody	62

Chapter 17...62

Special Circumstances and Child-Support 69

Chapter 18...69

Courtroom versus Mediation 78

Chapter 19...78

Create Lasting Peace 81

Chapter 20...81

Introduction

Women have been getting big wins for decades by doing no more than showing up. Those easy wins have caused them and their attorneys to assume a win from day one.

Ironically, in a modern courtroom, those historical easy wins are benefitting men.

By assuming a win, women and their attorneys are failing to properly prepare for their day in court. They show up to hearings with little evidence to support their claims, and nothing to counter solid evidence from their opponents.

The arrogance and complacency that's settled into the women's camp represents the perfect opportunity for men and dads.

My story demonstrates how a well-prepared man can do incredibly well in divorce court.

The variable aspect of divorces are the personality types of its participants. This guide describes a universal approach that will prepare you to handle all personality types.

You may be divorcing a reasonable, practical and fair woman, or an unreasonable, irrational and vindictive woman - it doesn't matter.

If you prepare for a disaster and then have nothing bad happen, it's rewarding. On the flipside, being fully prepared for trouble before it happens, is equally rewarding.

The non-variable component to divorces is that *time is of the essence.*

Your divorce will not wait on you to recover from shock, despair or sadness. There's no practice sessions or do-overs.

You're going to be single in the not-too-distant future. Seize this moment to focus all of your attention on the legal process that is set in motion. Hire an attorney (selection tips to follow), then partner with her to make her the strongest advocate possible.

Chapter 1

A Male's Perspective

When I began my search for information to help me *get in it to win it*, I came across a few books and sites that specified their purpose was helping men in midst of a divorce. However, when I looked at the content, the help they were offering wasn't help at all. They were either teaching men to be subservient, e.g., do nothing and accept defeat. Or, teaching strategies and coping skills to men in the midst of criminal legal issues that came about after they were served with divorce papers; not the divorce itself, e.g., no contact orders, arrest for breaking and entering, disturbing the peace…

The majority of the horrific legal issues that divorcing men face aren't divorce related. They are criminal charges that are mostly the result of moving out of their marital homes before their divorces were finalized.

Men who move out of their marital homes prematurely, as in immediately after being served with papers, are making themselves vulnerable to being abused and victimized by their wives and the criminal system.

Note: While it's true that divorce laws acknowledge men and women as equals, criminal laws don't. All a woman needs to do is accuse a man of any type of abuse, stalking, rape... and he'll be hauled into jail as guilty until proven innocent. Moving out of your marital home before your divorce is finalized increases the risk of such outcomes. Once caught up in that system, you'll have no time, money, or energy to fight for a proper divorce outcome. Instead, you'll spend all of your time trying to prove your innocence. That situation then develops a life of its own, e.g., she'll show the divorce court evidence of criminal charges against you. Remember, as a male, it's the criminal charges, false or not, that will forever imply that you're guilty.

Chapter 2

Divorce in Simple Terms

Divorce is a lawsuit between you and your wife that legally defines your futures.

Legal proceedings are all about strategy.

Each side is expected to fight for equal representation. Women and their attorneys love men who waste time hoping, wishing or imagining that they're experiencing a temporary rough patch. It's during those months that the process keeps moving forward, which ends up delivering a decree that favors women.

Frankly, much of what you'll be battling will be traditions and yourself.

Traditionally, many officers of the court and members of our society expect you to hand over the keys to your castle to the woman you're divorcing. Women and their attorneys rely on these traditions to keep men from asserting their legal rights in divorce court.

Believe it or not, you're at high risk of unwittingly complying with the aforementioned expectations.

Continually reassure yourself that in the eyes of American law, you and your future ex-wife are equals. Don't make yourself a victim to societal expectations. Remain unswervingly diligent to your endgame and you will get past these internal struggles.

Remember, women are as independent and capable as men are - any other view is the definition of misogyny.

Chapter 3

The Smiling Warrior

When I was a child, my neighbor visited Japan. Upon her return she gifted me with a small wooden carving of a smiling man who had a stringy thin beard dressed in a kimono.

On closer inspection I noticed that his hand grasped a sword tucked beneath his kimono. My neighbor told me that he was known as the Smiling Warrior.

I stared at her blankly until she explained that his story reminded her of me.

The smiling warrior was a samurai. A master swordsman trained in the art of war who, above all else, preferred peace. He greeted everyone he met with a warm and welcoming smile and treated them with the utmost respect. Everyone he encountered described him as a kind and loving man.

On occasion, someone misinterpreted the smiling warrior's kind demeanor as a weakness and they attempted to exploit it. It was during those times when the warrior emerged and delivered a deathblow from the sword tucked beneath his kimono.

Be that warrior, and if possible, hire a lawyer with the same qualities. Having a gentle and kind lawyer who is trained in the art of battle is much more productive than an abrasive argumentative type.

I found my lawyer by going online looking specifically for male client's reviews. I wanted a lawyer with a track record of being readily accessible who demonstrated the ability to accomplish successful financial and custody agreements for males. I looked for reviews that mentioned issues similar to mine, then scheduled an appointment to interview the top candidates.

Make it your priority to hire an attorney from the same county that your divorce will take place. If there's no option but hiring a non-local attorney, then be aware that you're losing home court advantage.

An out-of-town attorney is less likely to have a working relationship or track record with your county court officials. In addition, every time she needs to attend a hearing or deposition, her fees will include hundreds of dollars of travel time.

Hiring a local attorney is advantageous. She's frequently in and out of your county courthouse. While there she can submit required paperwork, saving you hourly and delivery fees. She'll also be interacting with colleagues who are associated with your case (colleagues who interact with each other on a daily basis work better as a team than out of towners).

I'm purposefully referring to your attorney as a she because I think males benefit from females representing them.

Here's my logic: Women often hire women attorneys to represent them. Perhaps they feel more comfortable sharing the intimate details of their lives with someone of the same sex, but their reason for choosing a female doesn't matter.

Men and women approach divorce from different perspectives. Therefore, when a man is pitted up against a woman, he'll do well to have a lawyer who understands the female mindset.

Your work doesn't end with finding and hiring the perfect attorney. Your active participation won't end until your divorce is finalized.

Use your lawyer to help you, e.g., if the judge is setting a deadline for your financials and you're aware of an obstacle, e.g., you have prior commitments that aren't flexible, or you anticipate it taking you more time to obtain copies during the proposed timeframe, then speak up. Have your attorney present your concerns to the court.

Judges are people too; they're open to reasonable requests and will do their best to work with you. On the other hand, keeping your mouth shut under the assumption that you're being polite, and then missing a deadline will infuriate your judge. Impress the judge by respecting their time and your efforts will be rewarded.

You may feel that some of the advice in this guide is overly cautious. In fact, some of the scenarios I'll present won't apply to you, your future-ex or your situation. Nonetheless… allow the information to flow. Don't get hung up on trying to relate to each and every detail.

I'll make you aware of issues that have happened to other men along with a universal approach to dealing with them. Use these universal defensive techniques to protect yourself, and if these issues never come up, then no harm, no foul.

Here's a real-life example of preparing for events that may never occur that are beneficial to all concerned. I've recently taken up high performance driving. The first thing I learned was that a safe track experience wasn't a random event.

Before strapping myself into the driver's seat and hitting the accelerator, I had to accept the fact that all of my actions and reactions needed to be purposeful. Taking off without planning for possible mishaps that might take place on the track is reckless endangerment.

Out on the track, seated in the passenger's seat is my instructor. If I don't do the right thing, he's strapped in his seat with no way out. If I spin out of control, he'll likely react by putting his head between his legs hoping that when we stop moving, it will still be attached to his neck.

The moral to this story is that being prepared and in control of the speed and direction of your divorce will be highly gratifying, while strapping in and going along for the ride is too risky.

Chapter 4

Universal Precautions

No one can predict with absolute certainty whether their upcoming divorce will be low or high conflict. That's because the experiences and stresses that lie ahead of divorcing couples are entirely new to them. Couples with a long history of treating one another reasonably and fairly are likely to conduct themselves in ways that are entirely out of character for them.

How do you think the average mild-mannered guy who's busily working to provide for his family will react when he's suddenly burdened by the expense and time-sensitive requirements of a divorce? The odds are that he'll be bordering on frantic, and that's exactly what his wife and her attorney are counting on.

The winning strategy of his future ex and her attorney are simple - keep this guy on an emotional roller coaster in all matters of finance, custody, and property division to the point that he's overwhelmed and confused. It won't take long for this dude to mistakenly believe that the quickest way to end his misery is to let the professionals do their thing, e.g., "I'll sign whatever you want. Please, let's just end this thing so I can get on with my life."

Ironically, when these guys anxiously and hastily sign away their rights to *get it over with*, the process still takes months to become official.

Guys… slow your thoughts down. In spite of your busy schedule and all of your current worries, there will be adequate time to accomplish all that will be required from you.

Chapter 5

Dress Me Slowly I'm in a Rush

You've just been served with papers for divorce, or you served your wife with papers - don't panic, there's time for you to learn.

Many men in your position think that the best thing they can do is to accept whatever their wife demands. Perhaps they feel the need to prove to their family and friends that they're a nice guy and a team player. Maybe they believe that choosing the path of least resistance will be less costly. Whatever their reasons, accepting whatever comes their way is a hasty plan that will result in significant long-term emotional and financial misery.

Gentlemen, your future, and if you have children, their futures will be affected by all that you do between now and the final divorce decree.

A well-executed divorce of a multi-year marriage may take 12 or more months.

Don't rush into making decisions that you'll later regret.

A quote attributed to Napoleon best represents what I'm emphasizing to you.

Napoleon was preparing to head into a raging battle when he advised his assistant, "Dress me slowly, I'm in a rush."

Napoleon's message was on point. He didn't want to hastily enter a battlefield then find himself in hand-to-hand combat only to discover that his sidearm was left back at camp.

Move slowly and purposefully while keeping your eyes fixed on the prize - a fair divorce.

Always keep in mind that your opponent is your former best friend. She knows your innermost secrets, strengths, and weaknesses.

She's anticipating zero resistance from a sad and broken man; not the proud and honorable man she married. Well... she's in for a surprise because you're going to be exuding the confidence of a champion.

Your confidence during divorce proceedings will piss her off and she'll likely lash out at you. No cause for worry, simply prepare for her wrath and everything will be fine.

No matter what she throws your way, always keep your cool. One slip of your tongue, loss of control, or angry outburst will cause accusations, e.g., "Look, see how angry and threatening he is? I've been oppressed by this horrible man for years!"

Don't fall victim to obstacles designed to make you lose your cool.

Until your divorce is final, picture yourself as a man being tried in a courtroom whose every word and action are being critically judged by a jury. The jury in your case is your wife, children, relatives, co-workers, attorneys and in the end, an actual judge.

No need to feel paranoid, simply remain hyper-vigilant. Assume that any situation that comes your way that would cause an average person to lose their composure is a trap to make you appear savage.

Remaining calm, cool and collected during the stressful days ahead of you isn't going to be easy. Should you have a slip of the tongue, don't overthink it. Simply offer a sincere and rapid apology to the person involved, regain your composure, then move forward with a clean slate.

Chapter 6

Happy Wife, Happy Life

The average guy, married or single, truly believes that their wants, desires and needs are irrelevant. They walk our earth like robots babbling, "Happy wife, happy life. Happy wife, happy life…"

Historically, women raise boys. They train boys to be subservient, reverent, and to elevate women to a status way above their own.

Indoctrinating boys to become chivalrous men is a brilliant method of controlling them. Men readily buy into the concept of being a provider, protector and guardian of the opposite sex - *it's the manly thing to do.*

There's nothing manly about being subordinate to women.

Conducting yourself in a chivalrous and misogynistic manner is flaunting an exploitable weakness in your character; a weakness that women and their attorneys take advantage of.

Wives learned that serving their husbands with divorce papers is likely all it will take to cause him to immediately move out of their marital home. The dude will actually leave all of his belongings behind.

Every day, previously levelheaded and responsible men get served divorce papers, then hastily abandon their lives to establish themselves in lifeless apartments. They throw away many of their rights long before stepping foot into a courtroom.

If they have children, they too are left behind. Undoubtedly, their kid's heads are spinning in disbelief wondering why their dad suddenly lost his mind and abandoned them.

Ask the guy who impulsively abandoned his home why he did so and he'll tell you that he moved out to *keep his divorce friendly for his wife and or children.* In his heart, this guy is convinced that his actions were the right thing to do.

Treating the opposite sex as weak when they're not, and throwing away your rights during a divorce lawsuit is insane – completely delusional.

Chapter 7

Remain in Your Marital Home

You've survived living under the same roof with your future ex during the time leading up to divorce, so there's no reason you can't remain there until your divorce is final.

If you're planning to move out prior to finalizing your divorce, then you'll be financially responsible for your new place. You'll also remain responsible for the marital home you left, along with half or all of its upkeep and maintenance.

Establishing then paying for a second household during a time when you might be paying $4,000 a month in legal fees for the next 12 months makes no financial sense.

If you have children, setting up a second household prior to settling your divorce sends a strong message to the judge, e.g., you accept your wife as the primary custodian of your children, and you're not going to be readily available to support them during the stressful times of divorce.

On matters of custody and spousal support. Let's assume that your wife is demanding that she be designated the primary custodian for your children. Also assume she's demanding future spousal support.

Imagine the difficulty you'll face when trying to convince a judge that you'd make a better custodial parent and that you can't afford her demand for spousal support after already proving to the judge that you're capable of supporting two households, while leaving her alone to care for your kids.

Judges are practical, straightforward people. It's your actions, not your intentions that do the speaking.

Let's assume your plan is to move out for purposes of *keeping things friendly* for your wife and kids.

Guys… divorce is a legal procedure that dissolves a marital contract. Two adults under the direction of a court or mediation center will divide their marital assets. When there are children or pets, they will write up a new contract called custody orders. Your children will not be physically present for these events.

Emotional sentiments such as friendly and unfriendly don't apply to inanimate contracts and paperwork.

I stress this because, time after time, I hear guys stating that they moved out and did little to represent themselves in order to "keep their divorce friendly for the sake of the children".

The best way to keep homelife friendly for your kids during your divorce is to remain by their side; in your marital home.

Keep routines alive, be available, be supportive, maintain rules and expectations, don't badmouth or argue with their mom.

It's neither friendly or in your best interest to suddenly exit a household that you were an active and integral part of. Everything you own and everything you do centers around your household.

Make a hasty departure then try going back to pick up a few things, look through and make copies of your family's financial records, retrieve keys for your storage unit, tools from your garage, collect family heirlooms from your childhood, or other items that you entered the marriage with (non-marital assets). How about popping in for your traditional weekly pizza night with the kids? *That isn't going to happen...*

Once you leave the marital home, you can't simply walk back in, nor can you selectively remove things. You'll need to make appointments with your soon to be ex who will likely come up with obstacles that won't make it easy for you. This process will anger you and empower her.

Meanwhile, while you're out of the house with your divorce unsettled, your ex will likely be badmouthing you to her friends and family - always in front of your children. The kids will see and hear their mom upset and crying. They'll assume that you're the cause of her being upset and that will cause them to resent you.

Do you believe that your future ex will defend your absence to your children? This is the perfect setup up for Parental Alienation Syndrome. That's when one parent turns the children against the other parent – difficult to prove and worse to be on the receiving end of.

When the time comes for the judge to assess parents for custody, they'll look at the routines of both parents during the 3 months leading up to the divorce, as well as, the time period during divorce proceedings.

A father who took an apartment will be viewed as uninvolved - one who essentially granted full custody of his children to his wife. If that same dad suggested taking his children with him to his new place prior to the divorce being settled, then he would be viewed as someone willing to uproot and wreak havoc on his children's routines, e.g., bus routes and day to day events that they're accustomed to. It's these pre-divorce routines where many children find solace while their parents work out the specifics of their futures apart. These same practicalities apply to family pets.

Chapter 8

No One is Perfect

Don't allow your past to define your future. The court will evaluate your current behavior; not your remote past. As such, your pending divorce is the perfect time for you to become the person you always wanted to be.

Most divorces take a year to finalize, so, if necessary, use this time to reinvent yourself. Don't allow anyone to convince you that it's too late to improve yourself.

If the police were involved in anything pertaining to your past, then get a copy of the police report and go over with it with your lawyer. Be prepared to discuss the incident and prove that your actions since the incident are worthy of praise.

The same applies to your future ex-wife. Obtain reports that include her, because unlike you, she might not have worked on rectifying her past bad behaviors.

Many folks, women and men alike, have substance abuse problems, anger issues, and untreated depression. If you fall into one of those categories, then change it.

Need therapy? Start. Need Alcoholics Anonymous or Narcotics Anonymous? Begin. Anger issues? Address them by enrolling in counseling.

If you weren't a model parent up until this point, then now is the time to begin. If you didn't make time for parent teacher meetings, or chaperoning field trips before the divorce, then do so now. If your work schedule won't allow you to physically attend parent-teacher meetings, then no problem. Communicate with your child's teachers through email. Ask if they can accommodate a video chat. If you can't chaperone, express it in an email and ask if there are other ways for you to pitch in to make their field trip a success. Create a paper trail that proves your involvement.

Chapter 9

Home-Based Strategies

Remain in the marital home until your divorce is settled, but always keep in mind that you're a male living with your female legal opponent.

Frequently remind yourself that all you do between now and the final divorce needs to be purposeful. Adhere to a non-emotional objective plan and you'll obtain the best possible outcome for yourself.

Set up your sleeping quarters away from your future ex. Tell her she's welcome to remain in the master bedroom. Set up a place for you to sleep in a guest room or living room.

Do your best to remove whatever you need from your prior bedroom so that you don't unintentionally intrude on your wife's space.

If you have a separate master bath in your home, move your toiletries to an alternate bathroom.

Arrange your new sleeping quarters and situate your personal belongings in the neatest, least intrusive way. If you're going to be sleeping in the living room, store your bedding in a closet during daylight hours, then bring it out when it's time to sleep.

If there's a family coat closet, swap the coats out to store your personal clothing.

Keep your home looking and feeling as pleasant as possible. Being sloppy will set you up for arguments and ridicule.

If you have children, tell them that daddy won't be sleeping with mommy any longer and they can expect to see you sleeping in a new location.

Sleeping away from and avoiding close quarters between you and your future ex is the easiest way to avoid conflict.

Let's imagine for a moment that your wife is not the sweetest person on earth. On top of that, she's feeling a bit vindictive towards you because she and her minions anticipated that you'd move out as soon as you were served divorce papers.

Your future-ex might decide to have you forcibly removed by making a false claim of rape or assault. She knows that in the face of zero evidence, based solely on her word, that the police will side with her, remove you from your home, and arrest you if she instructs them to.

The above might sound outlandish to you, but remember, the entire concept of getting divorced might have seemed outlandish to you a few months ago, yet here you are.

Keep a safe distance from your wife because once a man is accused of assaulting a woman, he's guilty until proven innocent. I'd much rather see you focusing on getting an equitable divorce than fighting to get out of jail.

Don't be scared of your circumstances. Rather, remain hyper-aware of your surroundings along with the potential risks you're exposed to during a contentious male and female relationship.

At this stage you may be thinking that the best way to avoid false accusations is to move out of your marital home. However, I continue to weigh in on the side of remaining home. Besides, moving out won't eliminate your risks.

Whether you remain in the marital home or not, every time you show up there's a risk that you'll find yourself starring in a nasty public scene.

Let's say you moved out then return to your marital home for an officially scheduled visit.

Or… you remained in the marital home and are returning from a normal work day.

You pull up, then suddenly your wife frantically runs up to your car screaming at you to stay away. Or, you pull up, park, then while walking up to the front door she blocks your path; gets in your face and screams. She might incite you to raise your voice, or move her out of your way. Her frantic behavior gives your neighbors the impression that you're doing something wrong.

The neighbors will testify as to what they saw. You can be arrested and be served with a no contact order that will keep you away from her and the kids.

Chapter 10

Prepare To Be Judged

This chapter is all about self-defense.

In New York it's legal to record and videotape interactions between you and your spouse. Consent is implied when just one of the couple are aware that there's a recording taking place, e.g., if you know you're recording something between you and your spouse, that's all the consent you need. Ask your lawyer to clarify the rules in your state.

The freedom to record is fantastic, and if you're in tune with your wife's behaviors and responses to stress, you'll have a huge advantage.

Prepare to capture moments when your future ex-wife will predictably be out of control. Set up nanny cams where you know she's most likely to misbehave to record all the action.

Maybe her favorite moment to let loose on you is after the kids go to bed while you're grabbing a snack in the kitchen. Maybe she likes to harass you when you're alone in the garage working on a project. If this sounds like your wife, the kitchen and workshop will be perfect locations to set up your nanny cams.

If your nanny cams go missing, it's no big deal. Always keep your smart phone handy and whenever you sense your future ex approaching your space, hit record.

Make it a habit to hit the record function on your phone whenever you arrive home from work/errands, or whenever you and your future ex are going to share a space.

Should your wife confront you about your nanny cams, remember, home security is perfectly legal.

Should she get angry and destroy your monitoring devices, then she's starring in a video that shows her illegally destroying spousal property.

The realization and possibility that one is recording the other is a win-win. You'll both be striving to avoid regrettable actions because you'll be conducting yourselves as if there's an invisible judge with a birds-eye view documenting everything you do.

There's also the real possibility that your wife won't have any strategy except anticipating you'll be like most males and let her have her way. This is especially true if she's a narcissist.

A narcissist will be so caught up in admiring herself and her abilities, accepting no responsibility for her actions, that she'll allow herself to be filmed acting as badly as she always had.

Recordings are valuable fact collectors, especially if your wife has a routine of badmouthing or emasculating you. Poisoning your children against you can result in her losing her bid for custody, as well as being denied contact with your children.

Should a situation arise that is down to a female's word against a male's, she's got the upper hand. If there's no recorded evidence, her word will be taken as fact.

Recording interactions between you and your wife will protect you from false accusations.

A final note on recordings: Install nanny cams on entrances and exits as well as where valuables are stored, e.g., important paperwork, the wedding silverware. If those items suddenly go missing, you can scroll through the memory to discover the culprit, then invite the police over to investigate the theft.

You'll likely never need them, but just in case events take a wrong turn, your videos can level the playing field - it's the "cover one's bases" philosophy.

Chapter 11

Interim Divorce Home Life

Be prepared for your wife, friends, or family to repeatedly suggest, and or pressure you to move out.

Have some fun with these non-supporters.

Respond to your friends and family in a matter of fact, non-sarcastic tone, "I don't mind if my wife moves out. I'll help her pack if she likes. In fact, she can move in with you."

Respond to your wife in a very kind and supportive tone, "If you feel strongly that it's best we separate until the divorce is settled, then I respect and support your decision. Let me know when you want to leave. I'll rent a moving van for you and help you pack it. Don't worry about us, the kids and I will be just fine."

Here's a scenario that can happen to you while remaining in your marital home: There were a few evenings when you were supposed to take care of the children so your wife could go to work. One of those nights, on the way home from work, there was an accident that caused a huge traffic jam. Once cleared, you had the misfortune of a flat tire from debris on the road - you didn't make it home in time. Two weeks earlier, you experienced a dead battery and were stuck in the parking lot at work.

For both incidents, you phoned your wife and kept her current.

How do you think your future-ex will describe those events?

This may seem farfetched, but your wife might decide to log both incidents on her calendar to later make and support a claim that you're routinely irresponsible at a future custody hearing.

Imagine the judge turning to you and asking if your wife missed work on two occasions because of you. You respond, "Yes, but… "

Now imagine you didn't keep your own calendar with a screen shot showing the calls you made to your wife, along with photos of the dated and timed receipts proving your car repairs.

This type of meticulous record keeping will save you and takes just seconds to complete with your smart phone. As such, anytime something out of the ordinary occurs, simply take a few seconds to log it.

You don't know what the future holds any more than I do, but should your wife decide to play the lying game, you'll have solid evidence proving the truth.

Chapter 12

Active Participation Matters

Your attorney will get paid whether or not she delivers a satisfactory outcome.

Liken your situation to a professional sports club. Every week, players from competing teams show up to play, then, regardless of the outcome, all players get paid. Teams with stronger coaches take home more wins.

Moving forward, picture yourself as a strong coach who hired a player with tremendous potential. Your player (attorney) is a seasoned athlete. She's an expert in all the rules of the game. What your player lacks is the inside knowledge and historical details that placed you in a position to hire her.

Think of it… your attorney just met you the day you hired her, then was immediately sent into the field with an expectation that she'll deliver a win.

The key to her success is your participation. Give her the evidence that made you who you are today to justify your defense, and then she'll bring home a win.

Some men take a passive approach to their divorce. They hire a well-respected lawyer, provide her with whatever she asks for, attend hearings, then sit back allowing their attorneys and judges to hammer out the details for them. Their logic seems reasonable, e.g., they're entrusting professionals who understand divorce law, so whatever they come up should be fair.

If you're planning to be one of these guys, then know this - laws dictate that all participants are treated equally, but they don't force you to actively participate and assert your rights.

A passive approach amounts to delivering crates of statements to your attorney, which without your interpretation and story, are as meaningful as putting them by the roadside on trash day.

Meanwhile... while you're passively handling your divorce, there's the possibility that your wife is actively participating. She's handing in statements as a form of evidence with stories attached that will help her attorney support her claims; that's *active participation*.

The outcome? Your wife will likely get whatever she requests as long as it's not illegal, because she actively participated in the process.

Following the above scenario to completion: Twelve months later, you're asked to sign the final decree. You notice that it states your son will spend every holiday and school vacation with your ex.

While you were busy working, your future ex proved that you didn't participate in family vacations and weren't festive enough during holidays. As such, the court concluded that it was in your son's best interest to spend those times exclusively with her.

The fact of the matter was that you avoided spending holidays with your wife because she was miserable and controlling.

You purposely requested working holidays and volunteered for over-time hours to avoid being in the presence of your wife. You believed your absence allowed your son to enjoy holidays more by not being in the presence of two miserable parents.

You also envisioned your future self, as a divorced man, finally able to enjoy holidays and vacations with your son. You assumed that the decree would simply divide holidays between you and your ex, because that's equality.

Regrettably, the court is unlikely to be empathetic towards your last-minute requests. As far as the court's concerned, your passive participation during the process was implied consent. Finally, if you think the holiday thing will be the only issue you discover to be unfair - then you're dreaming.

If you expect fair and reasonable decisions on your behalf, then you must actively participate.

Chapter 13

Divorce Threats

"Go ahead, divorce me and I'll take you for everything you have."

Threats like that are very effective at keeping a men married. Guys morph from husband into emotional hostages, all the time muttering, "It's cheaper to keep her."

Those are more than threats - women *have* been taking men for all they're worth - financially and spiritually.

Newly divorced women often flaunt their victories by hosting parties at their former marital homes. Tour her home and it looks the same as when she was married. Enter her garage and you'll find all of her ex's tools, cars, etc. The only thing missing is the ex-husband. He's off living in a tiny apartment furnished with charity shop furniture.

With stories like that, it's easy to see why men fear divorce.

However, there's good news for you.

Speak with the majority of unhappily divorced men, and it's likely that they hired an attorney, handed in what was asked of them, attended the hearings, then waited for the final curtain call. By no means were these men apathetic, they simply didn't understand that they needed to do more to protect their futures.

As a father of four sons who endured a long and miserable marriage, there was no way I was going to allow the system to be beat me to a pulp, then leave me with nothing more than the ability to breathe.

I planned to divorce on terms that gave my sons and me the ability to move forward the moment the papers were finalized, and that's exactly what we did.

Chapter 14

The Master of Details Wins

At its core, divorce is a process completely devoid of emotion that splits up a couple's home, assets and children.

While the process of divorce is highly emotional and demoralizing for its participants, it's important to keep in mind that in a courtroom, these are simply procedures; nothing personal.

Your judge will never ask you how you *feel* about your credit card statement from a year prior, or how you *feel* about a cancelled check. However, they will demand a full explanation for all non-routine purchases, so that they can assign the responsibility of that liability, or asset to the proper party, e.g., personal vs. marital.

Do not underestimate the value of putting in a tremendous number of hours into sorting out your finances for the judge. Separate your finances into two categories, personal and marital. Then, master the details of every item that passes through your hands.

While gathering financial information demanded by the court, do it with a sense of purpose and importance.

Create a list and paper trail that solidly assigns liabilities that belong to your wife, and that proves other liabilities are marital. Pay attention to liabilities that your wife might try to claim are yours alone (personal liability), because if successful, she's shifting what would have been 50% your responsibility (marital liability), to 100% yours.

Lets' say you find a charge for $4,000 that your wife previously hid from you and it turns out that you can prove it benefitted her and her lover - that's $4,000 in debt that won't be split fifty-fifty. The judge will hold her responsible for the entire amount. Maybe she's been living it up, taking solo vacations, leaving you behind with the kids while running up the charge card – that's her liability.

Many spouses take out loans during their marriage and for purposes of expediency, take them out under one name; not jointly.

If you have loans in your name only, but the proceeds of that loan benefitted you and your spouse, then be sure to prove that. Be prepared to counter your wife's claim that you alone are responsible for loans in your name.

Loans and credit cards are similar. You may have multiple credit cards in your name only, but all of the charges benefitted the marriage; not you alone. Create a paper trail proving that you both benefitted so that she can take 50% of the responsibility with her as she exits the marriage.

If you're self-employed and built your business after getting married, then the same principals might apply. Debt might be in your name alone, but your company was an integral part of providing for your family so it's likely to be considered a marital asset. It's likely that your wife participated in building and maintaining your business, so in many cases, 50% of the debt and assets related to your business will be assigned to her. As such, you'll want to avoid overstating the value of your business. Have your business carefully appraised so that it accurately reflects all depreciating assets and current market conditions. You'll want your business to appraise as low as possible because in the end, one of you might be buying out the other.

As a matter of routine, at the very start of your divorce, you and your wife will each be required to submit a list of assets. Make a very thorough list, then hand it into your attorney, but don't stop there.

Keep a copy of that list, then as your divorce proceeds, give each item on that list careful consideration as to its origin. Your goal is to claim ownership of as many assets possible for the final settlement day.

Importantly... keep this, and all of your financial strategies, entirely secret. Don't tell a soul. These lists are for your eyes only – protect them. The only time this information is to be shared with others is during the final accounting, on settlement day.

Prove and clearly delineate which assets are yours (personal). There will be many items that your wife will claim were acquired after the marriage that in fact you brought into the marriage. A wife will commonly claim that items you brought into the marriage were wedding gifts; not brought into the marriage by you. Many men consider such items too insignificant to bother protecting. Don't be one of those guys. Make it your goal to claim all that you can on your personal asset list.

Don't underestimate the thousands of dollars that you might gain by holding onto seemingly insignificant personal assets. Furniture, phones, computers, televisions, silverware and appliances add up quickly.

Let's say that you prove fifteen, $800 items are yours alone. That's $12,000 in your pocket - enough to cover several months in attorney fees. Left on the marital asset column, you'd be throwing away $6,000.

On the flip side, be ready to prove that assets your wife will try to claim as her own, are in fact marital – grab 50% credits whenever you can.

It won't be long before you're setting up your new home. Money will be tight, so you don't want to be buying all those items all over again.

Remember the lesson I brought up earlier – the litigant with the evidence wins. If you can show the judge reasonable evidence that an asset is yours and your wife has nothing prepared to prove you wrong, then you'll likely get the credit.

I've just loaded you up with lots of details that might have you feeling overwhelmed. Let's take a break and look at the process as something more general.

Judges and attorneys know exactly what's expected during a divorce; litigants are often clueless. Knowing what to expect, and what's legally expected from you, will calm your nerves on settlement day.

Let's imagine your judge as a professional baker instead of a judge. The job of your baker is to make a 4-layer cake with icing. In order to do their job well, they'll require specific ingredients, special pans, an oven, a timer, and in the end, they'll produce a cake.

The task of a judge in creating a proper divorce is the same as the baker baking a cake; both require specific ingredients to produce an acceptable outcome. Naturally, the cake will only be as good as it's ingredients.

A judge writes their list of demands - the recipe. You and your future ex provide what's demanded - the ingredients. The judge assesses and mixes the ingredients, sets a timer, and in the end, produces a divorce.

Breaking a marital contract follows a specific recipe whose ingredients are dictated by law.

No different from baking a cake, breaking a marital contract doesn't include ingredients of emotional breakdowns, depression, anger, or otherwise.

Provide your judge with poor ingredients and your divorce will not taste good.

Attempting to delay the process by making a claim that you're too depressed, or that the system is against you, won't alter the timeline that you'll have to hand in the ingredients.

Providing the judge with 1 egg instead of the 3 requested won't stop the process. The judge will make up for your deficits by using the ingredients provided by your future ex, and you're not likely to be pleased with that outcome.

Regarding your feelings and emotions: It's okay to be as dramatic as you want to be with those who support you, see a therapist if need be. However, when dealing with your lawyer and judge, keep your emotions at bay. For them, remain focused on providing all the meticulous details that they require to adequately represent your legal rights.

Your lawyer is charging you by the minute. Use her for her legal expertise, not as your therapist. Stick to the business at hand, save money, and win.

Chapter 15

Anticipate Betrayals

You'll experience many betrayals during your divorce.

Anticipate your soon to be ex to passively-aggressively poison teachers, neighbors, your parents and children against you.

These betrayals will be painful, especially coming at a time when you need the support of those you always assumed were your loved ones. However, as with most negative events, there's something positive to be gained from them.

By spending time poisoning others against you, your wife's helping you.

She's weeding out folks in your life who were not your true friends. She's wasting time that she should be spending on divorce preparation. Her actions are increasing the likelihood that you'll get the lion's share in your divorce settlement.

Ignore her, and anyone else with negative vibes.

Don't waste one minute trying to defend yourself, or winning back traitorous folks because it will distract you from collecting, documenting, organizing and presenting all that you need to come out on top.

Embrace the lonely road that you're on. Then, after your divorce, you can establish new and healthier relationships.

My description of the betrayal scenario may come across as flippant, but make no mistake, events not directly related to your divorce *will* zap your energy.

The losses I experienced were exhausting. There were moments when I thought, "If it's just money and things she wants, then take them. All I want is for this torture to end so I can get on with my life."

Fortunately, when those dark days arrived, I was purposefully keeping my circle very small. All of my interactions were limited to positive thinking friends and family; zero contact with all drama makers. My supportive friends and family lead me out of the darkness and kept me on course.

As time passed, I mourned the losses of those who betrayed me as if they were deaths. They're out of my life forever.

Any drama that your wife, or her minions try bringing into your life, are no more than desperate attempts to derail you from properly representing your interests - don't fall for them.

Your divorce won't take forever. Each day brings you closer to a glorious new beginning.

Chapter 16

Timing and Money Matters

Once your divorce is imminent, e.g., it's simply a matter of who serves whom and when, then do your best to get your wife to serve you. Further... get her to serve you at a time that is best for you, e.g., a time when all of your ducks are in a row.

Let's say the first part is done, e.g., your wife will be the one serving you, but you learn that she's going to have you served earlier than is ideal for you. In this case, plead with her to reconsider serving you until a later date. Feign desperation and appeal to her to hold off, e.g., a holiday is coming up, or your kids are prepping for finals and don't need the distraction of a divorce.

In the end, let her be the one to serve you because in New York State at least, the one who files for a divorce is the one responsible for the cost of the initial filing, as well as the final summary judgment (thousands of dollars). Ask your lawyer to explain the rules in your state.

The day I was served, I arrived home after dropping the kids at school and found a sheriff in my driveway. I parked, then with a big smile on my face, "Hi, I'm Richard Wood. You have divorce papers for me." The sheriff said that was the first time he was anticipated and greeted so warmly – I was ready and eager.

Timing is also critical when it comes to managing your marriage's largest asset – your marital home.

First off, don't make any property improvements because a home in need of love and upgrades will appraise low. You'll want a low appraisal when it comes time to divide marital assets.

Importantly: *When ordering a marital home appraisal, be sure to hire an appraisal service that was mutually agreed upon by you and your wife, then have your attorneys put that agreement in writing. If you don't take that precaution, then you risk being accused of obtaining a biased appraisal. In that situation, the judge might demand a new appraisal during the final hours, which will be costly and delay your exit. In my case, my wife and her attorney made that claim, but we immediately countered their claim* *by showing our judge the written agreement, and our case proceeded on schedule.*

It was awesome being prepared for my opponent's deviousness and equally nice to watch them lose credibility with our judge (he was visibly upset with them for playing dirty).

The back story was that my wife and I had no prior relationship with the appraisal company. In fact, our attorneys randomly chose the appraiser and neither of them worked with that company before.

Tip for appraisal day: *Greet the appraiser and if your wife is present, cordially introduce her. Next, provide a brief history of your home and property followed by a tour while pointing out the home's needs. Then, leave the appraiser alone to do their job. Remain available for questions, but do not hover.*

On the day of our appraisal, I pointed out that my home was a former foreclosure purchase with good bones that I had the intention of renovating, but financial circumstances brought all projects to a halt. I informed the appraiser that I never got around to paving the poorly drained gravel driveway, installing safety railings around decks, updating the kitchen, baths, replacing the 40-year-old windows that looked fine, but on closer inspection, didn't function well and had many air gaps.

You might think that the details I pointed out would be obvious to an appraiser, but appraisers often scan for a big picture. They check off boxes on a general checklist, such as, age of roof, age of HVAC system and so on, then submit the information into a computer for comparison pricing. As such, it's important to point out specific details that will decrease your home's value during a careful inspection of a future buyer, or mortgage company evaluation.

If you plan to remain in the marital home after divorce, then you'll be buying out your ex for half of the appraised value. Same rule applies if you plan to sell your half to your wife. In either scenario, maintain your home in such a way that it will appraise low. Investing in home improvements during a divorce is always a bad idea, especially since you're going to need lots of cash available to pay for the process.

If neither of you plan to remain the marital home, then this represents an awesome financial opportunity for you.

Tell the court that you decided to remain in the marital home and buy out your wife's half as part of the settlement.

You'll buy your wife out at the low appraisal – the house needs care value - then after the divorce is final, you'll fix it up, sell it, and pocket 100% of the profits. I did this then moved to a much less expensive market and sponsored a great new start for myself.

Something to avoid: Couples who don't plan to remain in the marital home, often make plans to sell the house as joint owners. Don't go along with that plan. I've met couples who took that route. Their homes became contentious burdens that tied the two together long after their marriage was dissolved.

There will be joint taxes, insurance, mortgage payments, maintenance, utilities, realtors – the list goes on. If it doesn't sell quickly, the two of you might consider making improvements. The entire process requires joint funding. In my experience, half of the couple, often the female, will refuse to come up with their half. Do you think that scenario will play out well between you and your ex?

If you don't have the cash to buy her out, then get a mortgage in your name. Do everything in your power to cut ties with your ex and set yourself up to profit later.

Buy the house, get the title and all the responsibility into your name. You'll be free of any drama, and can do what you like with it when your ex is no longer tethered to you.

Let's look at some numbers. Assuming the pre-divorce appraisal of your home came in at $180,000 and you're planning to buy your wife out. You'll buy your wife out for $90,000 (Mortgaged, or owned, the buyout amount is the same). After the divorce is finalized, you make improvements to the house with some elbow grease, and a $25,000 investment. After improvements, your new appraisal comes in at $300,000.

In summary: When your wife left, you owned a $180,000 home. You invested some elbow grease and $25,000. Now, the new value is $300,000 - your profit is $95,000.

Another tip: I owned a horse trailer valued at $4,000. I purchased it during my marriage so it was a marital asset. I initially planned to keep it and buy my wife out at fifty percent of its value.

However, as my divorce progressed, money got tight and I needed $4,000 in cash to pay attorney fees.

In New York State, I was able to sell that trailer for its full value of $4,000, then use the entire proceeds to pay for direct divorce expenses.

When the final divorce accounting came, the horse trailer was no longer on the books as a marital asset, or any asset at all. Perfectly legal, my wife didn't get $2,000 as originally planned, and I pocketed a net gain of $2,000. She literally paid some of my legal fees.

In the grand scheme of things, the trailer proceeds were small. However, the impact on the opposition was large, e.g., they got caught off guard, lost their cool, then failed to prepare for my next win.

Chapter 17

Children and Custody

Your approach to your children, like the divorce process, is best done by actively and consistently avoiding drama.

Always remain calm, cool and consistent with your children.

If prior to your divorce you would have denied access to a cell phone for a week from your child for receiving poor grades, then continue to do so.

Anticipate guilt entering your mind and playing with your emotions whenever you think about your children living in a divided home. Avoid the temptation of overcompensating, e.g., don't remove or relax the expectations that you have for your children.

Maintaining the routines and rules that you raised your kids with will reassure them that they can count on you to remain their usual trustworthy and reliable dad.

Should your kids suddenly and uncharacteristically begin breaking rules, or doing poorly in school, don't hesitate taking them to see a child counselor.

I normally wouldn't jump to a counselor right away, but during these stressful times, times when your wife is more likely to undermine your rules for no reason other than making herself appear as the nice parent, your kids can benefit from outside help.

Most kids are clever enough see the "nice parent" act for the manipulative action that it is. However, left unchecked, some might enjoy the insincere attention. They'll turn the situation into the game, then eventually move onto pitting you and your wife against each other.

Hiring a counselor as a support person for your kids, rather than trying to address the situation as a dad, when your wife isn't likely to support your efforts is a solid plan.

During my divorce, it became clear that my children could benefit from counseling but when I brought it up to my wife, she was adamantly opposed.

My lawyer informed me that I didn't require my wife's permission to take the kids to a counselor, or any other health care professional for that matter, so I booked appointments then sat the kids down in front of their mom to announce my plan.

Immediately after telling the kids that they'd be meeting with a counselor, my wife did all she could to derail my plan. "Come on kids, your dad's not making any sense. You don't need to speak with some scary old counselor. You know mommy and daddy are divorcing. Divorce is no big deal these days, so there's no need to waste your time with a counselor. I have a much better idea. Let's go and get some ice cream! I bet I can beat you all to the car!"

Trust your gut. If something inside of you is telling is that your kids would benefit from chatting with an outside, neutral and non-judgmental person, then make it happen.

Reassure your children that it's normal for kids to get off track when their parents are divorcing. Explain that divorcing parents don't always work well together and you're worried that their recent behavioral changes are signs that they're not getting a chance to share their personal feelings and worries.

Acknowledge that kids in their situation often feel the need to side with one parent over the other. Kids in their position often feel pressured to tell one or both parents what they think they want to hear, rather than what they're truly feeling.

Explain to them that you're their dad, not an experienced counselor. Let them know you're worried that you might be missing something that a counselor can easily help with.

"Kids, here's the deal. The counselor you're going to meet won't tell your mom or me anything you talk about unless she is worried that you might physically harm yourself, or others. Other than that, she'll keep everything you talk about to herself. If there's something bothering you, feel free to tell her because she's likely to teach you strategies that will help you feel better. I'm sure you noticed that I've been a bit preoccupied by my personal situation, but I'm not preoccupied enough to not notice that you're no longer doing well in school, or that we don't talk as freely as we used to. Seeing this counselor is a good plan. I'm convinced that you will appreciate what she has to offer."

Our kids might not think of asking for help on their own, so it's up to us as responsible dads to show them the way. If we fail to act on their behalf, they're at an increased risk of resorting to unhealthy coping mechanisms.

Do not fear sending you kids to an independent private counselor. These professionals are objective sounding boards for your kids. You select them and they help your kids work through difficult times. Don't confuse a private counselor with a court appointed counselor.

A court appointed counselor performs inquisitions, then dissects relationships, to find fault with one or both of the parents for the sole purpose of helping the court determine custody. They are not sounding boards for your children, nor are they child advocates. Court appointed counselors are notorious for placing children with mothers over dads, including with mothers who have a proven track record of child abuse.

In my case, the counseling and confidential conversations between my sons and their therapist turned out to be a huge benefit in the courtroom.

My ex and I were attending a court ordered Status Hearing. Our judge asked us where we stood on matters of custody. My wife's attorney stood up and began spouting lies about my behavior towards my children, including claiming that I was an unfit custodial parent.

My wife's lawyer knew that the court wouldn't bring the children themselves into the courtroom for their opinions, so she was resorting to discrediting me with lies and hearsay.

As previously mentioned, in the absence of proof, a female's word is often taken over a male's, but I was prepared for that event.

My attorney immediately presented the judge and opposition with the name and address of a credible witness – the boys therapist. In addition, she presented invoices and canceled checks proving the boys had multiple sessions during the year leading up to that hearing.

My attorney then asked the judge to subpoena the boy's therapist for an official summary of her findings.

My wife and her attorney sat in the courtroom with their with their eyes agog. Then after a few second huddle, my wife relinquished her custody demand for three of four of our sons.

The therapist never stepped foot into the courtroom, and in one glorious moment, I won sole custody of three of my sons.

My success was the result of persistent and proper preparation.

Chapter 18

Special Circumstances and Child-Support

Divorce for most men will be remembered as a low point in their lives. However, for a subset of men, divorce is the perfect opportunity to reorganize and improve the quality of their lives.

Family management is the same as managing a business. There's budgeting, networking, expansion, contraction, hiring and firing of employees, debt, property acquisitions, liquid assets, tax planning - you get the picture.

In the business world, when losses are too great to recoup, a business can file for Chapter 13 protection.

Chapter 13 is a reorganization bankruptcy process that discharges debt for a struggling business owner - a fresh start if you will. The businessperson gave it their best shot, but when all was said and done, their best shot wasn't good enough, so they're legally relinquished from all debt.

There are special divorce circumstances when a guy may want to consider filing Chapter 13 per se. For example, he managed his family to the best of his abilities but in the end, his best wasn't good enough.

What do I mean by special circumstances?

Perhaps you're a guy with a busy international career and or other time-consuming responsibilities. Spending quality time with your kids is impossible; nothing about you is a family man. You've always provided for your family, and you're not dissatisfied with the way your wife is raising your kids.

You might be a guy who's entirely different from the aforementioned businessman.

You're actively involved with your family, have a family friendly career, but there's a serious problem - your wife and children have no appreciation for your dedication and self-sacrifice. If you're this guy, and I ask you to describe two memorable and happy moments with your family, you'll likely be unable to recall a single joyful moment. In fact, your family has done no more than treat you like a doormat.

If you can relate to one or a combination of these guys, it might be best for you to avoid a traditional divorce.

Rather than taking the traditional route as a passenger in your divorce, grab the wheel and use your divorce as a vehicle to reorganize your life to start out fresh.

It's entirely appropriate for you to apply a piecemeal approach to your divorce, e.g., "I'll take this. Nah, that didn't work for me before and it's certainly not going to work for me as a divorced guy."

Just as you would during a traditional divorce, there will be a fifty-fifty split of marital assets with your wife, but rather than working out a shared custody arrangement, you're going to give her sole custody of your children.

Why? If you're the businessman, you've always been too busy, and will remain too busy to function as a family man. Giving up your right to custody is simply legally designating your wife as the person who will be 100% in charge of your children - no change from your married situation. By doing so, you've carved out and kept the financial responsibility you always had, but leave behind the unrealistic expectation of your future physical presence.

If the businessman above were to take the traditional approach, he'd have ended up with a divorce settlement that stipulated a 50% custody responsibility. No doubt, his ex would badger him to spend weekends and holidays with his kids - time he'll never have. His kids would become a source of strife between him and his ex - a disastrous situation for all concerned.

Next, let's assume that you're the unappreciated family guy. Divorce likely crossed your mind countless times but the old adage, 'it's cheaper to keep her', prevented you from pulling the plug. It was the fear of divorce - the fear that you couldn't afford to leave that kept you miserably shackled to your family.

Financially, there's great news for all types of guys - astronomical and subjective child support and alimony awards are a thing of the past.

The days of paying alimony to your ex-wife for purposes of maintaining her status as a housewife, a position she held during the years you were married to her, are over.

Gone are the days of chauvinistic misogyny. Women are now held to the same standards that men are. Women and moms are finally appreciated and recognized for their ability to work and earn a living the same as men and dads.

Another item in the win column for non-custodial parents is that most states adhere to specific formulas for determining child support. These formulas benefit the parent paying the support much more than the recipient parent.

Let's assume you have one child, live in the state of New York, and gave up custody of your child. You'll be ordered to pay the custodial parent 17% of your income until your child reaches 21. For two children 29%, 31% for three to four, and at least 35% for five or more children.

As the non-custodial parent, if you have a health insurance plan at work, you'll be required to maintain that for your children until they're 21. This might sound expensive, but co-pays, medication costs, dental care and all uncovered expenses are the responsibility of the custodial parent.

Consider the following scenario: You hand over custody of your two children and you're earning

$60,000 a year. You'll pay your ex $17,400 a year until your oldest reaches 21, then you'll pay the reduced amount of $10,200 per year until your youngest reaches 21. Imagine yourself living a single life, allowing your wife to raise your two kids while having between $42,600 and $49,800 to spend as you please.

The child support you'd pay covers everything - clothing, food, extra-curricular activities, baby-sitters, nannies, lessons, uniforms, sports, transportation, cars, licenses, insurances - you name it, that's all you're legally expected to pay.

That said, if at any time you'd like to hand over more funds to your ex for your children, e.g., for orthodontic work, vacations, college, then you're free to do so - it's a gift; there's no legal obligation.

Giving up custody does not mean no contact, or exclude the option of interacting with your kids - you're simply avoiding contractual visitation. Should your kids desire to hang out with you, vacation with you or anything else, they simply ask their mom.

Imagine being a fly on the wall witnessing the parting conversation between the unappreciated guy and his ex-wife: "Honey, the papers that you and your attorney served me with demanded that you remain in our home with our kids and pets. You've always said that I've done a bad job being a parent and our kids feel the same as you do. Look at it as you're all getting what you wanted. Really…congratulations, nicely played. Oh, and don't forget that the judge's orders state that you have six months to pay me for your half of our home, or it needs to be sold."

As a recipient of child-support, I can tell you that the amount I receive is nowhere near enough to cover the costs of raising my children. Funnily enough, my ex has not sent along any gifts to me, or our children.

Do I feel that child-custody payments are too low and unfair for me as the custodial parent? Absolutely no. I think that modern child-custody formulas reflect what the average person is capable of paying, without putting them into financial ruin.

I always understood that bringing children into the world was a huge financial responsibility.

Becoming a single parent with the privilege of sole custody of three of my sons meant I'd be going from a two-income to one-income household, and I would bear additional financial obligations.

Nonetheless, managing finances as a single-parent was much better than when I was married. As a married man, my wife treated me like I had access to a bottomless pit of money. Here's a typical conversation that took place in my home when my wife demanded money that didn't exist.

Me, "Honey, there's no more money, we're maxed out. If you want the kids to remain in private school then we'll need to cut costs. I'm happy to work with you, let's sit down and make it happen. How about decreasing our date nights to once, or twice a month instead of once a week? We'd save on dinners and babysitters. After 6 months we'd save enough money and can consider adding back more frequent date nights. Oh… a better idea. We hardly ever use our vacation home, how about we sell it? That place alone is costing us $2,000 a month."

Her, "That's complete bullshit. Why are you punishing me? How about you get another job!"

I don't miss those conversations.

As the custodial parent, should I decide that more cash is necessary for raising my kids, then it's up to me to put more effort into budgeting or earning.

Take home points: Laws don't mandate that dads or moms be available to their children 50% of the time, or any of the time for that matter. Laws in most states protect the non-custodial parent from paying more child-support than they can afford. Finally, should you decide to grant your ex-wife sole custody of your children, then take comfort in knowing that it's socially acceptable.

I hope the information in this guide has inspired you to approach your divorce on an equal playing field.

Remember, don't waste valuable divorce preparation time worrying about traditional roles and expectations.

When all is said and done, it will be clear that your needs, desires, expectations and future were just as important as your ex-wife's.

Chapter 19

Courtroom versus Mediation

A common misconception, I suspect the result of successful marketing efforts, is that using a mediator to settle your divorce is less costly, friendlier, and easier than going through a courtroom with a judge.

Mediation can be okay for a straightforward childless couple who works well together, and knows exactly what they want from their divorce. They simply need the legal system to check off all the necessary boxes then sign off on their agreement. I doubt you know many divorcing people like that. Besides, two lawyers can easily write up a dissolution for agreeable couples, then submit it to a judge because in the end, that's where the papers generated at the mediator's office end up anyway.

Mediation might look appealing to the uniformed. Participants don't require a lawyer unless they'd like one. Mediators themselves aren't required to be a lawyer. As such, they can offer affordable half-day and full-day rates rather than charging by the minute like lawyers will. The downside is that you all may leave the mediator with an agreement for the judge to sign off on, only to discover that what you all worked out wasn't legal. At that point, you'll likely hire lawyers and start from scratch in court.

Unlike mediation, a courtroom leaves little room for games, e.g., litigants can't keep coming up with excuses for delayed paperwork, reports and such. Deadlines set by the court are not soft, e.g., if by July 1st, both parties are asked to present a list of all assets, then that's what occurs. Mediation can have such a simple matter like that dragged out for years, e.g., one or both parties can continually come up with excuses as to why they can't determine assets by the deadline. In the end, the process of trying to divide assets and decide custody matters at the mediator's may go on for 5 years, leaving you, your future ex, and any children in a miserable state of limbo.

While by no means the intent, mediation lends itself to game playing, drama and nonsense. The type of nonsense that might wear you down and cause you to make concessions that you otherwise wouldn't have. If your wife is a narcissistic manipulator, and your mediator suspectable and gullible, then you're in for an awful ride.

Couples can spend years in mediation without ever reaching an agreement - thousands of dollars, thousands of days and nothing. There's nothing friendly or pleasant about that.

The courtroom will not tolerate insolent nonsense. If you or your wife claims difficulty in determining assets, then a forensic accountant will be assigned and a deadline set to present the required information.

The courtroom is an objective, no-nonsense, no drama venue with firm deadlines where in the end you'll walk away with a neat and tidy divorce.

Chapter 20

Create Lasting Peace

Your days away from closing this chapter in your life.

All that remains is reviewing papers that will be sent to the judge for a signature and your divorce will be finalized.

Your lawyer will hand you a stack of papers that in the moment, might appear as routine, e.g., "Just sign here and it's over."

You endured a lot to get to this point. As awesome as those words sound, I'm advising you that nothing is *routine.*

That stack of papers defines your future. They spell out financial agreements, custody agreements, child-support, alimony, palimony, and so on.

A clean start and trouble-free future will be determined by closing any open-ended stipulations that exist in your final decree.

Evaluate each stipulation carefully. Any time you see a statement such as, "both parties will come to a mutual agreement" on such and such an issue, do your best to spell out a solution.

Why? You didn't end up in divorce court by making joint decisions well with your soon to be ex and that's not going to improve. This is especially true if you're exiting a relationship with a manipulative person, e.g., any future issues that require a joint decision will give her the opportunity to manipulate you.

Imagine contacting your ex to make a joint decision. She might ask you to do this or that, berate you over something she heard, ask for money, invite you to a dinner with her, and so on.

It's in your best interest to have a concisely written divorce decree that eliminates future joint decisions as much as possible.

Granted, there will be some matters that need to be left open-ended. In those cases, spell out a strict timeline to reach a decision along with the specific legal process and remedy. Specify who will be responsible for the legal expenses that will result from a mutual impasse.

If you were granted a one-time cash award, or monthly child support at the time of the decree, then spell out a strict timeline as to when and how the cash will be handed over to you. Stipulate what will ensue if you're not paid by on time, e.g., non-receipt of monies by a specified time will be classified as a *default*. That stipulation frees you from the effort and expense of proving a default, and allows you to immediately initiate a legal collection process.

If everything wasn't spelled out and you weren't paid. You would need to establish a new paper trail to establish that she in fact owes you, didn't pay, was given an opportunity to pay, then take all that information to a court for a ruling.

You'll feel like you're divorce never ended.

If you're the custodial parent and she works for a company, then eliminate her personal involvement from the process, e.g., don't allow her to mail you a monthly check. Instead, stipulate that you'll go to the county to fill out the necessary paperwork that will result in automatic payroll deductions from her employer, that will be directly deposited into your account.

Best wishes to you: Richard Wood

Should you wish to contact me, please email: manlydivorce@gmail.com